OPTIONS TRADING PROFIT PLAYBOOK

Stock Options Trading Strategies Crash Course for Beginners to Start Swing Trading & Day Trading Options for Income from Home & Make Money Online!

KEN TURNER

Table of Contents

Introduction

Thank you for purchasing *Options Trading Profit Playbook.*

The following chapters will discuss all of the things you need to know in order to get started with options trading and making a profit from those options, whether you decide to work with forex, futures, commodities, or even the stock market.

There are many different things you are able to work with when it comes to the options market. And for those who know the market and understand how these options strategies work, there is a lot of potential profit with a minimal amount of risk in the process. This guidebook is going to help you explore the different parts that come with options trading so that you can start using this strategy and making money in no time.

The first section of this guidebook is going to take some time to explore more about options trading. We will look at what stock options are and some of the benefits that they can bring with them. We will also look at the fact that there are many different choices when it comes to types of options you can trade in, which can make the trading a bit more interesting. The first section will also help you learn some of the common words and phrases that will come in handy when you start to trade.

From there, we are going to move on to the second part of this guidebook, which will help us get a little deeper with options and look at how we can get our feet wet with this kind of trading. We will look at options pricing and some of the Greeks that are used in this kind of trading. We can then move on to some easy examples of how options trading will work, so you can get an idea of what you will want to do in some of the different trades, then we will explore some of the things you can do when it is time to reduce your risks in trading and to help you to stay on the winning side of the majority of your options trades.

And finally, we will move on to the third part of this guidebook. Here, we are going to take a good look at the top six strategies you are able to use in order to trade these options contracts. We will look at some of the most common strategies that work well with options, no matter which side of the line you may be on. We will also look at how to work with the bull call and put, the bear call and put, the long straddle and strangle, and even the iron condor.

There are many different trading strategies out there that you can choose to work with and most of them can be successful if you know what you are doing and have the right amount of money to get started. But when it comes to finding a choice for investing that is not going to cost you a lot of money upfront but can help you to earn a big potential income in the process, then there is nothing better than working with options. Take some time to look through this guidebook and learn the exact steps you need to work with in order to start seeing success with your options trading today. Options trading can be a bit daunting to anyone starting to learn how, but with the right tools, coaching method and the willingness to learn and take a risk – it can be a very rewarding experience. Once you experience reaping the fruits of your labor, you will be more eager to learn and take part in options trading.

With all of the choices of books on options trading that are available, thank you for choosing this one to help you get started with your own options trading. Make sure to leave a review if you find this book helpful!

PART 1

THE OPTIONS TRADING CRASH COURSE

CHAPTER 1:

~

What are Stock Options?

Options are one of the methods you can use in order to get started in the stock market. They are a choice, or the option, for an investor to either purchase or sell a security, based on how the market is going. You will look at the market and decide that you think it is going to behave in one manner or another, then you would purchase that option.

If the underlying asset does what you thought it would, you would exercise your rights to that asset on or before the expiration date. If the asset doesn't end up doing what you thought it would, you would choose to let it expire and do nothing with it. This can cause you to lose some of the premium that you put down, but it is much better than what would have happened if you actually purchased that asset to start with.

If you decide to purchase one of these contracts, you as the investor are going to get the right, however, you are not obliged to purchase or sell at a specific price. The buyer of an option is going to pay a premium for the privilege of being able to purchase that option or sell it at their strike price, as long as they do it before or on the expiration date that both agree to.

There is a certain amount of risk that can come with this though. You have to make sure you are making the right decisions with the things that you purchase, and how long you are going to be in this kind of market. It may seem like easy money to make, but if you don't know how to read the market in the proper manner and you try to stay in the market too long, then you could end up increasing the risk and causing you to lose a lot of money in the process.

When we look at stock options, we are looking at when the investor purchases the right, but not the obligation, to purchase or sell a stock at an agreed-upon price and date. If things work out the way that the investor plans, they will choose to purchase that option and complete their trades. But if something goes wrong, or the market chooses to go in a different direction, they are still able to walk away without having to purchase that option.

There are two main types of options that you are able to work with. The first is a put, which is when you bet on the stock falling. The second is a call, which is when you bet on the stock rising.

In addition, there are going to be two styles when it comes to options, including the European and the American. The American options are the ones that you are able to exercise at any time between the expiration and the purchase date. This means if you see that the stock option is doing what you want before the expiration date, you can go ahead and exercise it rather than waiting and hoping that it will work out and stay there until the expiration date shows up.

The less common option is the European one. You can only exercise these on the expiration date that you chose, which means they can carry more risk. If your option reaches the point that you want before the expiration date and then falls back away from that, you lose all of your money.

Not only are you able to use options to bet on whether or not a stock will rise or fall, but you can also choose a specific date when they expect the stock to rise or fall by. This date is going to be known as the expiration date. This is an important date to work with because it will help you to price the value of the put and the call, which we will call the time value, and it is going to be used in a lot of the pricing models that you do with options, including the Black Scholes Model.

The strike price is going to determine whether you would like to exercise your option or not. It is going to be the price that a trader or an investor will expect the stock to be above or below by their chosen expiration date.

Let's say you want to bet on IBM and your bet is that this company will see a rise in the future. To do this, you will buy a call for a specific month (any month you would like for your expiration date) and then you will pick out the strike price that seems the most reasonable for your needs. So, if you think that the stock of IBM is going to end up higher than $150 by the middle of January, then you would want to buy a January $150 call.

The next thing we need to take a look at is the contracts. These contracts are going to represent the number of options that a trader is trying to purchase. One contract, when it comes to options, is going to be the same as 100 shares of the underlying stock.

Let's bring back the example we just did above. For this one, the trader decides that they would like to purchase five call contracts. This means that the investor is going to own 5 January $150 calls. If they are right and the price of the stock does go above $150 by the expiration date, then the trader gets the option to exercise, in other words, they can buy 500 shares of IBM's stock at the $150 mark.

The neat thing here is that they are able to purchase the stocks at that price, no matter how much they may be worth at that time. If the stocks of IBM have gone up to $200 by that time, the investor would still be able to purchase them for $150. They could then sell them and keep the profit for themselves.

However, with options, you do not need to purchase the stocks if they don't do what you were expecting. So, if the price of the stock never gets above $125 the whole time that you have the option, you can let the expiration date go by and not purchase them at all. You will lose the deposit that you put down to start the trade, but that is a lot less than what you would have paid if you did go through and purchase the stocks for more than they were worth.

Another thing that we need to look at is the premium. The premium is going to be determined when we take the price of the call and multiply it by the number of contracts that we bought. Then multiply that whole number by 100.

Going back to our other example, if a trader purchased 5 January IBM $150 calls for $1 a contract, then the trader would need to spend $500. On the other hand, if the trader would like to bet that the stock is going to fall, then they would need to purchase the puts.

Options can also be sold depending on what kind of strategy the trader would like to use. If a trader feels that the IBM shares are in a perfect position and that they are going to rise, they can purchase the call. Or they get the option to choose to sell or write the put.

In the second choice, the seller of the put would not need to pay the premium but would end up receiving that premium. A seller who is working with 5 IBM January $150 puts would receive $500. Should the price of the stock go above $150, then the option would expire worthless, which allows that seller to keep the premium.

On the other hand, if the stock closes below that strike price, then the seller would need to purchase the underlying stock at that price. If that happens, you would end up losing not only the premium but the additional capital. This is because the trader is going to own the stocks at $150 per share, even though they were trying to trade at a level that was lower.

As you can see, there is a lot of potential that can come when we choose to work with options and use that as our investment vehicle. Learning how to trade in these stock options and use them for yourself can be a great way to earn money on the stock market, while also protecting yourself in the process.

The call option

One of the forms of options that you are most likely to use is the call option. This is the option that a trader uses when they want to purchase the asset rather than sell it. The buyer who purchased this contract is going to hope that on or before the expiration date, the stock price will go above a certain strike price so that they can purchase it for less and make a profit by selling to someone else.

With this in mind, the buyer is going to pay the price in the contract. If the value of the stock went up, then the price the buyer will pay is lower and the buyer wins. When you bet that there is going to be an increase in the value of your stock, this means you are going long on that stock. There are a few choices you can make when it comes to what you would like to do with the option.

You can choose to exercise your option to purchase the stock. You would get it for a lower price this way. From there, you can choose to hold onto the stock or you can sell it on the market. Since you purchased it for such a low price and the market has gone up, you will be able to earn a good income in this manner.

Another choice you are able to work within a call option is that you can close your position out. When it is time to close that position, which can be called trading out, you are going to do something known as offsetting the trade by selling the option that you bought in the first place. In this scenario though, you're never going to be the owner of that asset that is in the contracts.

Put option

The other choice you can make with these is to do a put option. This kind of option is going to give the buyer a right to sell, instead of the purchasing that we talked about, by the chosen expiration date. This is the opposite of what you are going to see with the call option, and many times, a trader will just avoid using this.

As it may seem, the buyer who is working with the put option is going to plan that the market conditions will go down and the price of the stock is going to decrease in between the time they start their contract and their expiration date. If they are right, then the investor is going to sell that stock at a higher price, even though the value of that asset is lower. This is one way that you are able to short the stock because you are placing the bet that the price of the stock, or its value, is going to decrease.

How to trade with options

Options, for the most part, are going to be traded on the major exchanges, just like you would with their underlying assets if you chose to invest in those outright. The options market does have some regulations with it by the Securities and Exchange Commission or SEC. You are often better trading with the regulated options because these can keep you safer and help you do better with the trades. With that said, there are some choices to trade options over the counter. These are unregulated and some investors see them as gambling, so it is better to ignore these.

To enter into the regulated market on a major exchange, it is best to go through a brokerage firm. As you advance through this a bit more, you can choose to do it on your own. But as a beginner, it is safer to work with a broker and learn the ropes and the best securities and more for options contracts. They do cost a bit more on the fees that you will need to pay, but it is so worth it.

One thing to remember with this though is that if you would like to try out some options contracts and you want to see how this process works, you will need to submit an application as a retail investor. This is because options can carry a lot of financial risks and your broker doesn't want to let an individual get in too deep with the trades that they are doing. Keep this in mind when you are ready to get started with trading in options.

Working in options is not going to be for everyone. There is a lot of time commitment that comes with this and, often, it is a lot harder than what people realize when they are first getting started. You have to learn how the market works and understand the differences between the call options and put options. You also need to be ready to take on some of the financial risks that can come with this trading choice. But if you are willing and ready to put in the work for it, then options trading can be a really profitable endeavor for you to work with.

CHAPTER 2:

∼

Why Options Rather Than Stocks?

I f you have looked into investing in the past, you can tell that there are a lot of choices you can make. You can pick from different companies to invest with and there are different strategies that work well too. But the main question we are going to focus on in this chapter is why trading in options is a better choice than trading in stocks.

Options are less expensive

One thing a trader may like when they choose to work with options instead of stocks is that the options are less expensive. Each contract for options is going to give you control over 100 shares of equity, but the cost of purchasing this contract, and that many shares, is nowhere near the same as what you would pay if you had to purchase those stocks outright.

When you do decide to purchase one or more of these contracts, you are going to pay a premium to enter into the trader. There are several factors that come into play to help us figure out what the premium is. One of those would include the underlying equities price.

Let's take a look at how this is going to work. We are going to work with a company that costs us $3429 in order to purchase 100 shares of that stock. But if you wanted to do an at the money contract with your options trading, you would be able to purchase those for just $69 instead. This makes it a lot easier for beginners to get into the market and see some success as well.

Options are going to work with leverage

Because these options are going to be cheaper than going out and purchasing the equivalent number of shares, the options will provide you with something known as leverage. This feature is going to allow you to collect the profits that are, in the best-case scenario, way out of proportion to the amount you initially invested in the contract.

Sticking with the example above, let's assume that the stock was able to raise itself by $40 by front-month expiration. This means that the shares are going to be worth $4000 now. This is a gain of $571 from the initial investment or a total of 16.7 percent.

Meanwhile, the call that you made earlier is going to carry six points of intrinsic value (this is the stock price of $40 minus the strike price that comes in at $34). This means that the contract is going to be sold for close at $6, or $600 since you are working with 100 shares. Therefore, since you paid $69 to get started, your profits are 870 percent of the initial investment. This is a huge improvement compared to what you would have got if you had just purchased the stocks outright.

The risk can be minimized

A lot of investors like to work with these options because these contracts are going to minimize the amount of risk that is felt, even if the trade does not go the way you would like. We will take a look at the example again, but in reverse, so we can see how this will work and what might happen if the stock does not behave the way that we had predicted.

Let's pretend you purchased the stocks and then, during your expiration time, they plunged. By the time that you got to the end of your expiration date, they did not go up and they have gone down by $25 a share.

If you had gone through and purchased the shares outright through the stock market, your stake would now be worth just $2500. In other words, if this situation had happened to you, then you would be out $929, which is 27 percent of the original investment. Plus, you are still exposed at this time to any more downside that could occur over time.

But, if you had done this with some option contracts, the risk would not be as high. Since you paid the $69 on the call, that is the most you are going to lose for the trade. Whatever the premium of that call ends up being, even if the stock goes so bad that it gets to zero, you will never lose more than that. While the maximum profit potential, in most trading scenarios, is going to be unlimited with the buy call, the maximum amount that you are able to lose will be limited to the initial net debit paid to open up the position.

You can throw some of the fundamentals out the window

If you have already spent some time investing in the stock market, then it means that you have learned how to research various permutations of the price to earnings ratio. This helps you to figure out whether a stock is undervalued or overvalued at its current rates so you can decide if the trade is the one that you want to enter into and spend your money on. It is also common for traders in the stock market to take a close look at the fundamentals of the position before they decide to enter into it.

For all of the reasons we have talked about in this chapter and even some more, learn to know that it is fine to throw these fundamentals out the window when you want to trade with the options. The fact is, these kinds of metrics may work well when you are doing the regular stock market, but they won't matter at all for the options trader.

Thanks to the lowered initial investment per stock that you are putting up, and due to the leverage that we talked about, you have a very simple goal when it is time to purchase a call option. Your goal with this is to get the share price to rise above the break-even point, which is the strike price plus the initial premium that you paid before the expiration date happens. If this does happen, then you will be able to collect the profits you earned before leaving that trade.

So, since you are not going to spend your time investing into the company over the long-term, you won't really need to work with the traditional metrics of trading because they don't have a lot of bearing on the analysis. You just need to be able to figure out whether or not the price of the stocks is going to go up or down from their current location before your expiration date.

As you can see, there are a lot of benefits that come when you choose to work with options and make them a part of your trading strategy. While there may be some reasons that investors choose to work with the stock market instead, options contracts make it easier to get into the market with lower costs, allow you to work with leverage, and can really maximize your profits while minimizing the amount that you could lose.

CHAPTER 3:

❧

Types of Options

One of the neat things about options is that there are a couple of different types that you are able to work with. This provides you with more choices when it is time to start investing and will ensure that you are able to get the right ones based on your needs, your chosen risk level, and the type of economy that is going on at that time.

Some of the different types of options that you can choose to work with will include the following:

Call options

Call options are going to be the contracts that will give the investor or the trader the right to purchase underlying security. They are able to do this at the agreed-upon price in the future, based on what the contract states and the chosen expiration date. An investor will choose to work with these call options when they think the price of the stock is going to see an increase in the future.

This means that the trader is going to see themselves as bullish towards the market when they enter the contract. There are three situations you may encounter when you hold onto a call option and these include:

1. In the money. This is when the stock price is going to be higher than the chosen strike price.

2. At the money. This is when the stock price is going to be equal to the strike price.

3. Out of money. This is when the stock price is less than the strike price.

Pull options

The next thing you can work with are put options. This is going to be the exact opposite of what you are able to see with the call options. The trader who has one of these options has the right to sell their underlying security at a fixed price at some point in the future. The investor who is working with this will purchase a put option when they think there is a high chance that the price of the stock will go down in the future.

Again, you can work within the money puts, at the money puts, and out of the money puts just like you can with the call options as well.

American style

Despite what you may think when you first get started with this one, it actually has nothing to do with the geographical area. Normally, when you have an expiration date on an option, the trader has to wait until that date arrives in order to exercise their right to buy if they are doing a call, or sell if they are doing a put contract.

The American style option is going to be a bit different. This option type allows the investor to purchase or sell the underlying security any time up to the expiry date. So, if it reaches the prices that they want, they are able to complete the contract and earn their money.

The main advantage of this is that if the market does do what you want, you are able to get out right away. You don't have to hold onto the contract and hope it doesn't go back down. This is a great thing for those who would like to limit the amount of risk they take on.

European style option

This is another type of option that you can go with, and the option holder is not going to have the same kind of advantage as we see with the American style. If you are the one being the holder in this style, then you are able to exercise your right to buy or sell only on the date of expiration. You do not get to do any of this at any time before that date occurs.

This is the main difference that shows up between the European and the American style option. Since there are going to be some limitations involved though, this is a less expensive option compared to some of the others, but there is some more risk working with this.

Exchange traded option

Another form of an option you can work with is known as the exchange-traded option. This is going to be a standardized form of an option that can sometimes be called the listed option. What this means is that any option that is listed on a public traded exchange will fit into this category. You will find that this option type is going to be the most common among the options traders. It is one that any trader can use.

Over the counter option or OTC

You can also work with options contracts that have been traded in the OTC market. This is not the same as the exchange-traded options that we talked about before, and for the most part, it is going to be less accessible to most retail traders and investors.

If you do find an option that is under this category, it simply means that the option has been traded by two private parties and has been customized according to the needs that these two parties have. It is possible that you may see the OTC option listed as a dealer option as well.

Option types based on their securities

The stock option is one that a lot of traders like to work with. When we are talking about one of these options contracts, the publicly traded shares are the ones that will most likely come to mind. Fewer people have an idea that there are other types of underlying securities that they have available and can choose from when they are looking on the market.

With that in mind, it is important to note that there are different types of options based on the kind of underlying security that is with that contract. Some of these will include:

1. Stock option: This is the most common type of contract for options. This is when the underlying asset is going to be shares of a company that are publicly traded.

2. Index option: This is going to be pretty similar to the stock option above. But the big difference is that the underlying asset is going to be some kind of index instead.

3. Currency or forex options: This is when the underlying asset of your contract is going to be a specific currency. This will give the one who holds onto the option the right to either purchase or sell at a fixed exchange rate.

4. Commodity options: With these, the underlying asset is either going to be a physical commodity or a commodity futures contract, depending on what you would like to trade.

5. Futures options: With this kind of option, the one who holds onto the contract has the right to enter into the specific future contracts with a fixed price, at any time that they want before the expiry of the contract.

6. The basket option: And finally, there are also those that are known as basket options. These are going to be based on the group of underlying securities.

Types of options and their expiration dates

It is also possible to take the options and list them based on when their expiration is, or at least their expiration cycle. There are some kinds of contracts with options where you will only be able to use them with one type of expiration cycle. And then there are some where you are able to pick out the expiration cycle that works best for you. Some of the different types of options that you may work with based on their expiration cycle include:

1. Regular options: This is the standard. You are going to get options for four different months of expiration while also purchasing the type of options contract. You will be able to use your preference to choose the expiry months that you want to work with.

2. Weekly options: With this contract, you will see some similarities with the regular options, but the expiry period is going to be shorter. You will usually only be able to use these with some major indices or limited underlying securities.

3. Long-term expiration anticipation securities: This is going to be a contract that lasts for a bit longer, but it will always expire in January. It can last somewhere between one to three years.

Cash-settled options

These are a bit different than the other options we have talked about. With regular options, the investor is either going to buy or sell the underlying security when the contract is over. But when you work with the cash-settled option, the way to settle this will be different. With this one, the contract is going to be settled with cash, rather than transferring the securities. The one who wrote the contract will pay the profit in cash to the one who holds the security. Because of this, these options are used when it would be really hard or cost a lot to transfer the underlying security.

Employee stock options

When we are working with this kind of option, a company will give their employees the right to purchase a number of shares from that company at a fixed price. And they usually have to do it by a certain date. This is used as a benefit by a lot of private and public companies in order to compensate, retain, and attract more employees.

This is a bit different compared to some of the other option types you can work with. This is just offered to the employees who work for that business. The employees will get this as a type of benefit and can decide to purchase or sell the stocks as they wish.

Exotic options

And finally, it is possible that you can work with a type of options contract known as exotic options. These have features that are often more complicated than normal options. Exotic options are going to be over the counter in most cases, instead of being exchanged on the stock market. It is even possible to customize these based on your own needs.

Because there are some investors who love to work with these exotic options, it is becoming more common for a few of them to get listed on the exchange, although most are not. Some good examples of exotic options that you may have heard about in the past can include chooser options, compound options, barrier options, and binary options.

These are some of the most common options available for you to try. They are meant to add some variety on the security, and even the timing, of your trades, which gives you a lot more flexibility than you are going to be able to get with any of the other trading and investing choices.

CHAPTER 4:

❧

Learning the Lingo

Now that we have looked at some of the different aspects of the options contracts and how to get started with options trading, it is time to move on and learn a bit of the lingo that comes with this kind of trading. These are some of the terms that you are going to hear as you move through this guidebook, and having a full understanding of how they work from the beginning can make a world of difference. Some of the key phrases and terms that you need to know include:

Liquidity and volume

The first terms that we are going to discuss are liquidity and volume. When we talk about volume in the options trading market, we are basically referring to how many transactions are being made that involve a contract. If a specific contract is bought and sold often, or heavily traded, then it is going to have a high volume. If it is not sold and bought often, then the volume is low.

The trading volume of the contract is important because it will affect liquidity. There are some other factors that can come into play, but this one is important. The liquidity of the option measures how easily the stock or the underlying security can be traded at its market price. If you see an asset that is highly liquid, this means that it is easy to buy and sell that asset.

Bull markets and bear markets

These are two types of markets that you may find yourself, or a particular asset, under. They are pretty much the opposite of each other, so we are going to take a bit of time to look at them.

When you are in a market financially and you notice that the prices of the stocks and assets in that market are rising, or are expected to rise in the near future, then you have found yourself in a bull market. When you see a financial market that is experiencing some falling prices, or it is expected that the prices are going to fall, then you have found yourself in a bear market.

Whether you are currently in a bear or a bull market is going to really affect the type of investment you are doing, and will help you determine what kind of options contract you should go with. The strategies that you use for each one are not necessarily going to work for the other type of market conditions, so knowing what kind of market you are in from the beginning can be critical.

A fundamental and technical analysis

These are the two main types of analysis you will do with an asset before you try to pick out one to purchase contracts with. All of the strategies that you work within options trading will fit under one of these categories, so knowing what they are and how to use them is very important.

To keep things simple, the fundamental analysis will be all about carrying out some research on security in order to figure out their inherent value. This one won't necessarily take a look at the price on the charts and graphs. Instead, it tries to figure out what the value on the management, reputation, and other intrinsic things will be and how likely it is that others would purchase that stock at a later time.

The biggest reason that investors are likely to choose this kind of analysis is that they want to be able to figure out whether a stock they are interested in is overvalued or undervalued. They will look at who runs the business, the financial strength of the business, the current and upcoming products and services of that company and other benefits and disadvantages of this company that could influence the actual price of the security.

Then there is the technical analysis. This is the one you will use when you spend time looking at charts and graphs to figure out the trends with security that you want to use. This one assumes that anything and everything that would affect the price of the stock will be found in the charts and so it assumes that the fundamental analysis may not be that important. You will spend time looking over charts and graphs and figuring out which kinds of trades you would like to work on based on that.

The contract size

One common issue that you may run into is a misunderstanding of how big a contract size is in options trading. They assume that one contract is going to be the same as one unit, or one share, of the asset. However, most of the contracts you will use with options are going to cover multiple of that underlying asset. So, if you purchase a call option in one company, it may mean that you are purchasing 100 shares in that company.

The number of shares that are covered in the contract will be called the contract size, and for the most part, this is going to be 100. You should double-check ahead of time so you know how much you are purchasing. The size of your contract is going to determine how much you will end up paying for it, and the underlying assets if you choose to exercise that right.

Moneyness

To keep this one simple, moneyness of an options contract is able to define the relationship that shows up between the strike price of a contract and the current price of any underlying security that is covered by that contract. The moneyness of your chosen contract can be in the money, out of the money, and at the money, as we discussed before.

The price of the contract is going to be related to its state of moneyness, and this is really important while you work on which trading strategy you would like to use. Because of this, understanding where it fits in and how to use it can be so important when it is time to start trading.

Leverage

One of the neat things that come with working in the options market is that it allows you to use leverage to your advantage. Leverage is going to be when you can multiply the power of your starting capital to increase the size of your potential profits in the process. Because options work in a certain way, you can use these to effectively invest in a larger number of stocks or any other security that you are working with than you might have been able to with just purchasing that underlying security outright.

Margin

The use of margin in your investment is a bit complicated. This is mostly because there are a few meanings that come with this and it will be different depending on the type of investment you choose to make. This can be enough to confuse even experienced investors, much less those who are just getting started out.

Margin or trading on the margin allows you to basically borrow money from the broker in order to get into the kind of trade that you want. You will then be able to purchase more of the contracts and potentially earn more money. If you make an accurate prediction, you will earn enough to cover the amount you borrowed from the broker and any fees they ask for, along with enough to ensure that you get to keep some profit in the process as well.

This becomes dangerous when your predictions end up being wrong. If the market does not go in the manner that you had predicted, you will lose a lot of money. You still have to pay back the amount that you owe to your broker, along with their fees and any money you put up front for this as well. This is why, especially if you are a beginner, it is best if you just stick with the money that you can afford to lose.

Options tables and options chains

Reading the options tables that are available to you can be important when it comes to trading. This is because these options tables are going to show you the relevant information you need regarding the various contracts that you may want to purchase or sell. There are actually a few ways you can use this information based on what you are trying to glean or learn from them. These tables can either be option chains or option tables.

Time decay

When it comes to trading in options, it is important to be careful about the time decay. This is the idea that the extrinsic value of your contract is going to start diminishing as you get closer and closer to the expiration date. The effect of this time decay will cause a significant impact on the returns that you are able to make when you trade in them. That is why it is so important to understand the time decay and how it is going to affect your trades.

The options premium

This is a term that even some more experienced investors are going to run into trouble with. It has been used over time to mean a lot of different things, and sometimes it is used in the wrong manner, so it is basically accepted in most circles that the term has more than one meaning.

One meaning that you may hear often is that it is the price that is paid for the options contract you want to purchase, or it is the extrinsic value component of that price, of the amount received by the writer of the contract.

The strike price

When we are talking about the strike price, we are talking about the price per share where the investor is going to purchase, when they are working on a call option, or sell, when they are working with a put option, and the underlying asset they are working with.

Exercise

This is going to be the process by which the investor is going to invoke the terms of their contract. If they choose to exercise it, the calls are going to decide to purchase that underlying asset. The put owners are going to sell the underlying stock under the terms that were set by the option contract. When you are working with an options contract that is considered in the money (which means that they are going to have an intrinsic value of at least one cent), at expiration, they are going to be exercised automatically for you.

Hedging

Hedging is a strategy that works well when you want to keep your risks low and want to work in a more conservative manner. You will use this to reduce the risk of the investment by doing a transaction that is able to offset the existing position you worked with.

Covered call

Another thing to know a bit more about here is a covered call. This is a call option that is written or sold against the stock position that you already have in action. The call is going to be covered by that underlying asset, which could be delivered if you decide to exercise your new call option.

Long and short

When you are going long on an option, it means that you went in and purchased it in the first transaction and then you have to own or hold onto it. If you go short with your option, it means that you have sold the option in the first transaction. This kind of position is negative on your statement and you will need to purchase it later to get the whole thing to close out.

PART 2:

GETTING OUR FEET WET IN TRADING

CHAPTER 5:

❧

Options Pricing: Understanding the Greeks

Many investors in options contracts will learn how to rely on the Greeks in order to help them get a good evaluation of their options positions and also to help them determine the sensitivity that comes with those options. The Greeks are known as a collection of values that are used in order to figure out how much risk is involved with any given contract of options based on how that risk will relate to underlying variables. Some of the most popular Greeks that you may use in your trading are Delta, Vega, Gamma, and Theta. Sometimes you may also encounter Rho depending on the types of trades you decide to work with.

Delta

Delta is one of the most popular options you can use with Greek. It measures the amount of sensitivity there is to the price, based on the price changes of your chosen asset. This could also be known as the number of points that this price is going to move each time you see one point change in that asset. Delta is an important Greek because it can provide you with a good indication of how much you will see that the option value is going to go up or down in regards to the changes that occur in the price of that underlying instrument. It makes the assumption that all the other variables you are using will stay the same.

Delta is going to be shown as a type of numerical value that falls somewhere between 0.0 and 1.0 for any call options, and 0.0 and -1.0 for all of the put options.

Vega or the sensitivity to the underlying's volatility

Vega is the Greek that can measure how sensitive the option is to the changes in volatility that happens with the underlying. It also represents the amount that the price of the option is going to change in response to just a 1 percent change in the volatility of your underlying. The more time you have before the contract is going to expire, the more impact the increased volatility will have on that price.

Because having more volatility implies that the underlying is going to go through a lot of extreme values, a rise in this will increase the value of the option. Of course, if there is a decrease in the volatility, it will end up affecting the option value in a negative manner.

Gamma or the sensitivity to the delta

Now we are going to take a look at the Gamma. This is the one that will measure how much sensitivity there is to the Delta when we look at the price changes with that asset. It can also show us how much of a change in the Delta will happen when there is just one point price change in that asset.

Since we already explored how the value of Delta changes at a variety of rates, Gamma is going to be used in order to measure and then analyze the values that you get with Delta. Gamma is often used by investors in order to determine how steady and stable the Delta is for one option or another. If the Gamma value is higher, it indicates that the Delta is more likely to change when it responds to smaller or bigger movements in the asset's price.

When we look at the Gamma, we will see that the at the money options are going to have a higher Gamma, but the Gamma is lower for the out of the money and the in the money options. The values of Gamma are often going to start out small when you are far away from your expiration date. And options that have these longer-term expirations will be less sensitive to the Delta changes. But, as you get a bit closer to your expiration date, the values are going to be bigger because the changes in the Delta start to have a bigger impact.

Theta or the sensitivity to time decay

Remember that we talked in the previous section about time decay and how it can eat into your profits if you don't plan things out ahead of time? The Theta is going to help you measure how much time decay is present in an option, or the theoretical dollar amount that the option is going to lose each day that time passes and you still hold onto the contract. Remember that, with this one, there is the assumption that the volatility and the price of the underlying will stay the same.

Theta will increase with any of your options that end up being at the money. They will then decrease when options are in the money and out of the money. Long puts and long calls will usually give you a Theta value that is negative. Short puts and short calls are going to give you a Theta that is positive. In comparison, an instrument that hasn't seen its value erode over time, such as with stock, would end up with a Theta that is zero.

There are a variety of analysis platforms and other online calculators that you can use in order to figure out what the current Greek values are for any of the options contracts you would like to work with.

Being able to read these charts and knowing fully what each of these Greeks do can make a difference in the kind of trading you are able to do. They will help you figure out what kind of options contracts you go with, whether you should go with a put or a pull option, and so much more, ensuring that you are able to get the most out of the options contracts you choose to work with.

CHAPTER 6:

~

Simplified Examples of Option Trading

O ne of the best ways to learn how to get started with options trading, or any kind of trading for that matter, is to take a look at some of the examples of other investors who have given it a try. Seeing what worked for them and looking at some of the real numbers can make a big difference when it comes to how successful you are going to be with the whole endeavor. Let's take a look at two of the examples you are able to work with when it is time to start your own options trading in the process.

John's example of trading

Let's say that John has decided to purchase an options contract. He purchases 1 Citicgroup Inc. on June 21 call with a strike price of $50. With this, they are going to pay $4 per contract when this stock was trading at the price of $49 a share.

At the same time, the trader then decides to work with the bull call spread and will sell 1 Citi June 21 call with a strike price of

$60, and they are going to receive $1 per contract at the time because the trader paid in $2 for their call and then received $1 for the put, the net cost to create this is $1 per contract of $100.

If the stock ends up not going up and falls short, then it reaches the price of $50 or below, both of the options are going to end up expiring and being worthless in the process. The trader will take a loss which ends up being the premium of $100 that they had paid in the beginning.

This is much better than purchasing the stocks outright. If you had purchased the stocks at $50 and then they fell by just a few dollars to $48 per stock, then you would lose out on $2 per stock. And since the contract is going to have 100 shares in it, you would end up losing $200. This is a big difference, especially in such a small amount of change in the stock.

Now, it is possible that the value of the stock could increase when you are in this kind of strategy. If you are working with this example and you notice that the stock increases to $61, the value of the $50 call that we did before would rise to $10, and the value of the $60 call would remain at $1. However, any of the other gains in the $50 call would be forfeited and the trader's profit on the two call options would end up being $9 (this is the $10 gain minus the $1 for the net costs). And since the contract is going to have 100 shares in it, you are going to come out with a profit of $900 from this.

Julie's example of trading

Now we need to take a look at another example of trading that can show us how to get the work done. This time, we are going to spend some time looking at how to work with an options trade that focuses on the bear call spread.

Let's assume we are looking into options and we see that there is a stock that is currently trading at $30. Julie finds that they want to purchase one call option contract. They do this and set the strike price at $35 and the cost premium at $50.

Julie then wants to sell one of the call option contracts that has a strike price of $30 for $2.50 or $250. In this scenario, if the price of your underlying asset closes below the $30 when the expiration date happens, then the profit of the investor is going to end up at $200.

The profit they are able to get from the bear call spread is going to max out in this situation when that security closes out at $30, which is the lower of the strike prices we are working with when we get to the date of expiration. If it is able to close at an amount below $30, this is great and proves that you made the right prediction, but there won't be any additional profit that you are able to get from this.

In addition, if the asset ends up closing between the two strike prices that you set up, there will be a profit still, but that profit is going to be reduced compared to the stock closing at $30 or below. However, if the asset ends up closing higher than that strike, such as at $35, then you are going to end up losing. The amount you will lose will be whatever the distance is between the two strike prices, reduced by the amount of the credit you got when the whole trade started for you.

CHAPTER 7:

~

Staying on the Winning Side

B efore we look at some of the different strategies you are able to use in order to make money with options trading, it is important to understand what steps you can take in order to ensure that you are always on the winning side and that you won't take on more risk than necessary. As a beginner, it is easy to take on a lot of risks. You aren't sure what steps you should take to see results with your trades, and you may get overly excited about what you are able to do with your trades. But with the tips below, you will be able to keep on the winning side, no matter what kind of contracts you choose to work with.

Not understanding how leverage works

Most beginners won't really understand how all of this leverage works, and so they will misuse it and not actually get the benefits. They will end up increasing the amount of risk they take when they do this. They may be drawn, for example, to work with short-term calls. Since this happens so much, you have to consider whether outright buying of the calls is going to be a conservative or a speculative strategy.

The best way to work with leverage is to start out slow. If you are used to trading 100 shares or less, then only do one option contract at a time. If you are used to trading 400 shares, then stick with four contracts. This allows you to see how the leverage works compared to your usual trading, and you can adjust once you get more comfortable.

Always have an exit plan

If you have been in the trading and investment market for some time, this will be something you have heard a million times. When you are trading anything, even if it is something that cuts out the risk like options contracts, you need to make sure that you add in an exit plan. Even when you see that things are going the way you want, you need an exit plan. Choose both a downside and an upside exit point, and the timeframes that you want to stick with when it comes to both exits as well.

Some people don't like to do this because they worry about getting out of the market too fast. Yes, there are times when the profits could be a lot higher. But isn't it a lot better when you are able to make more consistent profits, reduce how often you can lose money, and sleep better at night?

Never trying out a new strategy

There are too many traders in options, and other strategies, that will swear they would never do one strategy or another. They have one or two that they like and they will never switch from any of these. This is kind of silly. While it is a good idea to have a few strategies that you are fond of using, it is best to be open to a lot of different strategies because they are really going to serve you well.

Trading options that are not liquid

The liquidity of security is all about how easy and quick it is to purchase or sell that security, without it causing a bit of price movement. If you are in a liquid market, it means that you have lots of ready and active buyers and sellers when you will need them the most. To put it another way, this liquidity refers to the probability that the next trade is going to be executed at a price that is similar or equal to the last one.

While you are able to work with any kind of security that you want with an options contract, you will find that the stock market is the most liquid of the options. Stock traders just work with one stock but an options trader is going to have lots of options contracts to work with.

You want to pick out markets that are liquid and easy to purchase and sell. This may add to the volatility that you are dealing with, but it is much better than purchasing an asset and then finding out you are not able to sell it at all, much less sell it for a profit. If you get stuck with this, you are likely to either take a loss from the premium or lose even more in the process.

Waiting for too long of a period to purchase back your short options

This mistake is one that all traders need to keep in mind – and that is, as a trader, the opportunity to purchase your short options will always be there, therefore, you should always be willing and ready to commit to that. Taking too much time is an added risk. Many traders are going to end up waiting too long to purchase back their options once they have sold them. There are a lot of reasons for this, but some of the reasons are going to be:

1. You don't want to have to pay in another commission and potentially lose out on the profits you will earn.

2. You think that the contract is going to expire and when it does, that contract is going to be worthless.

3. You were hoping that you would be able to get just a bit more profit out of that trade.

You do not want to wait too long in order to purchase back those short options. If you do, you could end up losing out on a lot of money, and even lose all of the profits that you could have earned if you had gone through all of the steps in the proper manner.

Factor in what can happen in the future

It is true that you won't be able to foresee all of the different events that occur in the market. However, there are a few times when you will be able to foresee what is happening. There are two crucial events that you need to keep track of when you are ready to trade your options, and these include the earnings and the dividend dates for the stock you choose to work with.

For example, if you have decided to sell calls and you notice that there is a dividend approaching, then this is going to increase how probable it is, you may be assigned early if the option is one of the money options. This is especially true if the expected dividend is going to be large. The reason for this is because the options owners will have no rights to the dividend at all. To collect on this, you need to be able to exercise the option and actually go through and purchase the underlying stock.

This means that you as an investor always need to consider any of the upcoming events that could cause issues or could benefit your investment. For example, you need to know the ex-dividend date. Also, you should make sure that you don't sell any contracts for options with the dividends pending unless you want to have a higher risk when you get assigned.

Trading during the season for earnings means that you will end up with a higher amount of volatility with the underlying stock you want to use. And this also means you are going to pay a price that is pretty inflated for your option. If you would like to purchase your option during this earnings season, one of the best alternatives you can use is to purchase one option before you sell another. This helps you to create a spread.

There are no guarantees that come with trading in options trading and there are times when the market is not going to do what you would like at all. But if you do the following steps, and you learn as much as possible about these options contracts before you start, then you will be able to see a consistent amount of stress as you go.

PART 3:

THE BEGINNERS OPTION TRADING STRATEGY GUIDE

CHAPTER 8:

❦

Strategy 1 – The Iron Condor

Most investments are made with a good expectation that the price is going to go up. However, there are some that are made with the opposite expectation that the price is going to start moving down. What often happens though is that the price doesn't move a lot at all. There are some exceptions to this and you may see some big spikes up or down, but for the most part, a stock is going to be pretty steady. The good news is that you are able to work with the iron condor with options and still make money, even when the market isn't moving.

Iron condors do take a bit of time to learn, but they are great because they will be able to help you make profits on a consistent level. In fact, some of the best traders are going to use iron condors for most of their trades. This brings up the question of what an iron condor is.

The investor is able to take a look at the iron condor in a few different ways. You could look at this as having a short and a long position for the trade. Or you can look at it as a type of credit spread that will have two different parts. You will have a call credit spread that you will need to place above the market, and then you will also put a credit spread that goes below the market. The two wings that are formed with this ensure the iron condor is going to have its name. You are able to put these quite a distance from their place on the market, but if you are sticking true to this strategy, it is going to involve some strike prices that are consecutive.

A credit spread is a good strategy for option selling. This allows the investor to take a bit of an advantage when it comes to how that time premium works, along with any of the volatility that will show up in your asset. This credit spread is going to be created when you decide to purchase an out of the money option that is far, and then you sell a nearer and more expensive option in its place. This will help you create credit.

The hope with this one is that both of the options are going to end up expiring worthless so that you can keep the credit that you earn in there. As long as you make sure your underlying asset doesn't end up going over the strike price of the closer option, you get the benefit of keeping the full credit.

There are a few things that you may want to keep in mind when you decide to work with this strategy. The first one is that you will want to stick with index options for the most part. These are going to give you enough of the implied volatility you need to earn a nice profit, but they aren't going to have enough volatility that could end up wiping the account out quickly.

Another thing you need to be careful about with this one is never taking a full loss on this strategy. If you are able to pay attention and keep up with the math, you may notice with this one that any potential loss you earn here can be higher than your potential gain. This is going to make the trading strategy one that carries more risk than the others.

The reason this happens is down to the probability that you are going to be correct, if you spent the time watching the graphs and numbers that are presented to you, so your potential profits are not going to be so high. But the probability of you being wrong is low, so when it happens, your potential risk can be really high.

To ensure you don't end up taking on the full amount of the loss, if you see that the market is moving in the way that you think it would normally, and you see that the trade is staying in the range that you chose, then you can just let the trade continue on without making any changes.

You as the investor can decide to let the position expire without exercising any of your rights and just let it be worthless. When this does happen with one of your contracts, then you get to keep the whole of your credit. If you notice that the market has a strong preference for one direction or the other, and it starts to approach or break through one of the strikes that you have, then it is time to exit that position on that side to avoid too much in terms of losses.

There are a lot of ways that you can choose to get yourself so that the iron condor is done. One of the options investors can use is to sell their spread for the credit while holding onto the other part of this strategy. Or you can decide that you are done with this trade and remove yourself from the trade of the iron condor. The choice is going to depend on when your expiration date is and how long you have left with that contract.

One other method that you are able to try out to help with this is to roll the losing side so that it becomes an even deeper kind of strike for out of the money.

There are several different possibilities that are available for you to choose and the beauty of working with this strategy is how well you are able to manage your risks. If you can make sure that you work with this side, then you will be able to add a lot of the risk factors, like probability, and put them on your side.

When you work with the iron condor option strategy, you will find that this is a good way for any options contract to end in a profit when the asset moves at price. This one needs to be reserved though because it is most effective when there is a larger price movement, whether this goes up or down, in order to actually see the profits that are wanted.

The structure that comes with the iron condor strategy can seem confusing, but that is mostly because of the way we are used to doing our trades and the mindset that we already have. This could also be why only more experienced traders seem to work with it at all. But if you take some time to practice with it, maybe on some fake trades before investing any money, you will see just how great of a strategy it can be for you.

CHAPTER 9:

❧

Strategy 2 – The Long Straddle/ Strangle

The next kind of strategy we are going to focus on is the straddle and the strangle. To learn how both of these work, we need to get a better idea of how these are alike, and how they are different. The strangles and the straddles are both going to be strategies to use with options contracts. They will allow the investor to benefit from some big movements in the price of the stock, and they can work whether the price of the stock ends up going down or up.

Both of these approaches need to come with the same expiration date to work with. The difference between the straddle and the strangle is that the strangle is going to have two different prices for the strike, and the straddle is going to have a strike price that is common.

The Straddle

First, we are going to take a look at how you can work with the long straddle strategy. The straddle trade is just one way for a trader to earn a nice profit on the price movement of their chosen asset. An example of this is when a company has scheduled to release some of its current earnings for this quarter in the next three weeks. You know they are going to release the information, but you have no idea whether the news about the income is going to be bad or good for trading.

For the few weeks that happen before you get to the news release, it is time to consider working with a straddle. This is a good thing because once the results release, the stock is going to have a sharp turn in one direction or another. It is going to spike up quickly if the results are good. But it is going to spike down if the results are bad.

Let's take a look at an example of how this can work. Let's assume that the stock you are working with is trading at $15 in the month of April. Then suppose that the $15 call option for June is going to come in at the price of $2, and then the price of the $15 put option for June is going to be $1.

When you are working with a straddle, you will be able to see this turn into reality when you buy both the call and the put for a total of $300. This is when we add the $2 and the $1 and multiply by the 100 shares that will be found in your options contract. The straddle is going to end up increasing in value.

You will notice that the profits realized from this strategy will work as long as the price of the stock ends up moving either up or down, depending on the news that the company releases, by more than $3 per share in either direction.

The Strangle

Now that we know a bit more about how to work with the straddle position, it is time to take a look at another similar strategy, but one that works differently enough that it is important to take note of. Another approach to options is known as the strangle position. While the straddle is not going to have a bias in one direction or another, a strangle is going to happen when the investor believes that the underlying asset is most likely to move in one specific direction, but they want to limit the amount of risk they are dealing with and would like to add in some protection in case there is a negative move.

Let's take a look at an example of this. Let's say you are waiting for a company to release its information about income and profits and you are pretty sure that the results are going to be positive. Because of this, you will need less protection of a downside than before. This means that you do not want to work with the straddle as much.

Instead of buying the put option with a strike price of $15 for $1, you may consider buying at the $12.50 strike price, which will cost you $0.25. This trade would cost less than the straddle and also requires less of an upward move for you to break even. When you work with that lower strike put option with this strategy, you are still going to have some protection as needed against the unexpected if the stock does tend to go down fast. It also ensures that you are going to be in a much better position to gain from that positive announcement you are waiting for.

Special considerations

There are a few different special considerations that you will need to remember when you are ready to get started with these. First, you have to be careful with the tax rules on these because you are possibly losing money and gaining money at the same time.

In the past, some traders who worked with these options strategies would be able to manipulate some of the loopholes of tax in order to delay paying capital gains tax. This is a strategy that the IRS no longer allows. In the past, traders entered offsetting positions and closed out the side that was losing by the end of the year so that they could report a loss on the taxes.

The current loss deferral rules say that an individual can deduct a loss on a position only to the extent that the loss is more than any unrecognized gain the person has open on offsetting positions.

Any of the unused losses will be treated as sustained in the next tax year.

The straddle and the strangle positions are great strategies to work with when you are working with some options contracts. They allow you to be prepared if you don't know what is going to happen in the future for your position, and they can really help to limit your losses or increase your profits if you are certain which direction the underlying asset is going to go. Learning how to use these will make a big difference in how well you can complete your trades.

CHAPTER 10:

~

Strategy 3 – The Bull Call Spread

The next kind of strategy we are going to look at is known as the bull call spread. This is an options trading strategy that has been designed so that it can benefit from the limited price increase of stock. The strategy, when used in the proper manner, will use two call options in order to create a new range. This range is going to consist of a strike price that is lower and another strike price that is higher.

This kind of spread, which is known as a bullish call spread, helps the investor to limit the amount of risk and the number of losses that they get for owning the stock, but it ends up capping the amount on the gains that you are able to earn as well. This one has some give and take. You reduce the losses and the risks, but you also reduce the gains you can make.

This bull call spread is going to allow you to work with a lot of different underlying assets for the call options that are available. Some of the ones you may work with are going to include currencies, stocks, bonds, and commodities to name a few.

The basics of the call option

The call option is something that an investor uses when they would like to benefit and earn profits from any upward moves in the price of an asset. If it is exercised before the expiration date, then the trading options will make sure that the investor is able to purchase the shares at the agreed-upon price at the beginning, which is called the strike price.

The difference between options and futures though is that the investor does not have to purchase those shares if they don't want to. If they find that the stocks or assets are not moving in the manner they want or had expected, then they can let the option contract expire and will just lose their premium. But if they find that the movement upwards was favorable, then they are able to purchase the stocks at the lower price and take the profit when they sell.

When you are working as a bullish investor, you are going to pay out a fee upfront, which is the premium, for the call option. The premiums are going to base their worth, and the amount of price that you pay on the spread that occurs between the stock's current price in the market, and its strike price. If you find that the strike price of that option is near the current market price of the stock, then the premium is going to be much higher. The strike price is the price at which the option gets converted to the stock at expiration.

Now, if you do one of these kinds of contracts and the underlying asset you choose to work with ends up going below your chosen strike price, then it makes sense that you as the trader won't buy the stock at all. This saves you a lot of money in terms of what you would have paid for the stocks in the first place. But you will lose out on your premium if you choose to go with this option. If the share price does go up, the holder can decide to purchase shares at the price, but they can change their mind and not do this if they choose. In this case, as well, the holder is going to lose out on the premium that they had paid in the beginning.

You have to pay attention to how much the premium is, and then determine whether or not it is worth doing the call option. If the premium is high, you will need to see the price of the stock go up quite a bit in order to offset the amount you pay in premium. The break-even point is what you need to concentrate on.

The broker you choose to work with is also going to charge you a fee for placing an options trade, so you need to make sure that this is an expense that you will factor in to how much you are spending on the trade. Also, when you are pricing these contracts based on 100 shares or more, you need to remember that cost as well.

Building up your bull call spread

The next thing we need to look at is the steps we will take to build up the bull call spread. This kind of spread is a good one to work with because it reduces the cost of your call option, but there is a trade-off. The gains in the stock's price can also be capped off with this, so there is a limited range in where you as the investor will be able to actually make a profit. The trader is going to be able to use this kind of spread if they believe an asset will rise moderately in value, most often when you are going with a time that the volatility is high.

When you work with the bull call spread, there are going to be a few steps to work with, which involve working with two call options. The steps you can work with here are going to include the following:

1. Choose the asset that you believe is going to see some appreciation over a set period of days, weeks, months or another timeframe that you would like to use as your expiration date.

2. Buy a call option for the strike price that ends up being higher than the current market with a specific expiration date. You can also pay the premium here. This is going to be known as the long call.

3. At the same time, you want to sell a call option at a higher strike price that has the same expiration date as what you did on your first call option. The name we are going to give this one is the short call.

When you sell one of the call options, the investor is able to get a premium from someone else. This helps them to offset the price that they are going to pay for that first call. In practice, the difference between the two call options is the investor debt, which ends up being the cost of the strategy.

The next thing to focus on is how you are going to be able to get profits from the bull call spread. The losses and the gains you are able to get with this strategy are going to have some limitations because you have the upper and the lower strike prices. Upon its expiry, the amount of the stock declines below the lower of the strike prices, which is the first call option that you purchase, the investor is not going to exercise on that option. The option strategy is going to expire and be worthless here, and the investor will end up losing the net premium that they had paid at the beginning.

They do not want to exercise the option in the case above because they would end up having to pay more, which is what the strike price they selected is at, even though the asset is currently trading for an amount that is below that selected strike price. This just results in you losing more money than before.

If you get to the expiration date and you see that the price of the stock has gone up and it is trading above what you set for the upper strike price, the investor is now going to benefit by purchasing it at the lower strike price. This allows them to buy the shares.

This is a good thing for you. The price of the asset is going to be higher, so you can purchase them for less. You will then need to go out there and sell the stocks for the higher price. And if it stays there for long enough to do this, or you see the amounts go up even higher, then you are going to be able to take the profits that you earn.

However, the second sold call option is still going to be active at this point, and we can't forget how to work with that one. The options marketplace will automatically assign or exercise this call option for you. The investor is able to sell the shares that they bought with the first, and the lower, strike option for the higher, second strike price. Because of this, the gains that were earned from buying with that first call option are capped at the strike price of that sold option.

The profit you are able to earn here is going to be the difference between the lower strike price and the upper strike price. You then have to take away the net cost, or the amount that you ended up paying for the premium when you entered into that trade.

With the bull call spread, the losses are going to be limited quite a bit. This is a great thing for a new investor because it will reduce the amount of risk involved since the investor is setting themselves up to only lose the net cost they incur during the spread. However, there is a downside to this. Because you are limiting the risks so much, you are also going to be limiting the number of gains that you are able to make. This may be worth it depending on the amount of risk that you are willing to take, and it is a good way for you to learn more about trading and reading the market before you start to work with the riskier strategies.

CHAPTER 11:

❧

Strategy 4 – The Bear Call Spread

A nother strategy you can choose to work with is called the bear call spread. This is a strategy that you will want to use when you think that the underlying asset is going to have a price decline. It is achieved when you purchase the call option at a strike price while also selling the exact same number of calls, all of which have the same expiration date. But the ones you sell will have a strike price that is lower.

The maximum amount of profit you are able to gain with this strategy is going to be the same as the credit you can receive when you start with the trade. This means that you most likely won't make a huge profit, but at least you are able to make some kind of profit on a down market, a type of market that most people assume is hopeless.

The main advantage of working with this one is that the net risk of this kind of trade is pretty low. Purchasing the call option with a higher strike price can ensure that your risk is offset a bit. It is also going to carry a much lower risk compared to shorting the security because the maximum loss is going to be the difference between the two strikes reduced by the amount credited or received when you initiate the trade.

One thing to keep in mind with this one is that there is theoretically an unlimited amount of risk you could deal with if you end up guessing wrong on your predictions. For example, if you do the bear call spread strategy and the market ends up going up on you, then you can take that much risk, which can be as high as the market goes up by.

If the trader is looking at security and believes that the security is going to fall by a very limited amount between when they start to set up the trade and the expiration date, then the bear call spread is one of the best strategies for them to work with at this time.

On the other hand, if they do this and find that the underlying security ends up falling by a greater amount than what the trader had assumed or guessed in the beginning, then the trader has to give up their ability to claim any additional profit that comes up. This is a hard thing to work with, but it is the trade-off between the risk and the potential reward. And sometimes protecting your investment and not risking too much is the most important thing you can do in this situation.

The bear call spread is going to be a strategy where you make a purchase of two call options. The first one is a short position and the second one is a short position. These need to come in at different strike prices, but you need to give them the same date for expiration.

The bear call spreads are going to be considered a limited reward and a limited risk strategy to work with. This is because the investor will be able to contain the losses or even realize a reduced amount of profits with the help of this strategy. The limits that can come with the losses and the profits are going to be determined based on the strike prices that you decide to do with your call options.

This is a great strategy to learn because it ensures that you are able to get into the market and even make a small profit (it is more limited than some of the other strategies when it comes to the amount that you make), even when the market or that particular stock is going down at the time. This one may limit some of the profits you are able to earn, but it also ensures that you are able to limit the amount of risk you take on as well.

CHAPTER 12:

~

Strategy 5 - The Bull Put Spread

Next, we will look at the bull put spread strategy. With this one, the options investor is going to work to write a stock put so that the investor earns an income from the premium they pay, and maybe even to purchase a stock of their choice while getting it at a bit of a discount. A big risk of this strategy is that it obligates the investor to purchase the stock at the strike price, even if the prices end up going quite a bit lower. This means that the investor, if they don't do this the proper way, will result in a huge loss.

The nice thing about a bull put spread is that it mitigates the inherent risk that can come with put writing, because you will make a concurrent purchase of puts at a lower price. This helps to reduce the amount but it can also lower the amount of risk you have when you do the short put position. This makes for a more sensible choice considering the circumstances wherein the amount is reduced but the stakes or the risk remains high or higher.

A bull put spread is going to be when the investor will write or short sell a put option. At the same time, the investor is going to purchase another put option, working with that exact same asset. This one will have the same kind of expiration date, but the strike price is going to be lower.

This kind of spread is one of the basic types when we look at vertical spreads. The other three of these vertical spreads are going to include the bull, the bear put and the bear call spread. The premium you are going to receive for the short put part of this spread is always going to be more than the amount that you paid for the long put, as long as you do this process in the right manner. Therefore, initiating this strategy means that you are going to receive a credit or a payment upfront.

The neat thing about this one is that you are able to use it in order to make profits in several different manners. But first, we need to consider some of the situations where you would want to use the bull put spread. Some of these include:

1. To earn some premium income. This situation is going to work with the bull put spread because it is the optimum situation when both the trader and investor can earn maximum income. But along with that maximum income, the stakes would be much lower so it will be a win-win situation.

2. To help them lower the price they pay for a stock. A bull put spread is a good way for you to purchase the desired stock at a price that is more effective, one that is lower than the asset's current price on the market.

3. To help them to capitalize on a sideways or a marginally higher market. This kind of strategy is great for when you see that the asset is trading on a sideways chart or it is just a bit higher. Some of the other bullish strategies would not work well with doing this at all.

4. To help you earn income even if the market is choppy. But writing can be risky when the markets start to slide because there is a higher risk of being assigned stocks at prices that are too high. A bull put spread is able to help you write puts in markets that other strategies are just not going to work that well in.

To see how the bull put spread is able to work, we need to take a look at a few examples. Let's say that we are working with a company called Bulldozers Inc. This company is trading at $200 right now, but an options trader thinks that it is going to start trading at $203 in the next month. They would add puts on a stock so they can buy it at a lower price; they are concerned about the risk of the market going down.

To help out this risk, the trader is going to work with three differ-ent contracts of the $200 puts and this needs to be at $3, all expir-ing in one month. This means that the trader is going to purchase three contracts of the $197 puts, trading at $1, that also expire in one month. Since each of these options contracts is going to represent 200 shares, the options trader's net premium income is going to be $600.

Keep in mind that we did not include commissions in this be-cause we want to keep it simple, but there may be some other fees and costs that you are going to need to deal with in the process.

Now we need to take a look at some of the possible scenarios that could happen a month from now in the final minutes of trad-ing on the option expiration date. In the first one, the Bulldozer Company will have their stocks trading at $102.

In this scenario, the $97 and the $100 puts that you wrote ar going to be out of the money and will end up expiring pret worthless. The trader is going to be able to keep the full amou of the $600 net premium minus the commissions that come in scenario where the stock trades above the strike price of the s put leg is the best possible case for you when you are wor with the bull put spread.

The next scenario that we can work with is that the Bulldozer company starts trading at $98. In this case, the $100 put is going to be in the money by $2, while the $97 put is going to be out of the money, and this makes it worthless at expiration.

The trader is going to have two choices at this time. The first one is to close the short put leg where it is at $2. The second choice is to purchase the stock at $98 in order to fill their obligation for exercising the short put. The former course of action is the best option because if you do the latter one, you are going to end up paying more in commissions.

Closing the short put leg at $2 is going to entail an outlay of $600. nce the trader got a net credit for writing these at the beginning 500, the overall return that comes with this is going to be $0. ader is going to break even. But this is going to be much an what would have happened if they chose to work with al stocks instead of with commission.

ou could see a third scenario happen. With this one, is going to trade at $93. In this case, the $100 put is money by $7, while the $97 is going to be in the loss on the position is going to be $900 in this were able to receive the $600 at the beginning put spread, your loss is $300 instead.

The advantages of the bull put spread

There are many benefits that can come with the bull put spread. First, the risk is going to be limited to the difference between the strike prices of the long put and the short put. This means that there is not going to be as much risk of getting a huge loss in the process. This is something that traders who are working with other strategies have to deal with, but the bull put spread can help to limit a lot of the risk that you have to deal with. In short, the bull put spread limits the risk you have to face with options trading.

The bull put spread is able to take advantage of time decay. This is a very potent factor when you work with an options strategy and it is worthy to take note of as a very effective strategy as well.

You are able to work with this strategy in order to pick out your own risk profile. A conservative trader may decide to narrow their spread when the put strike prices are going to be close together. This helps them to limit the risk as well as the amount of money they could potentially earn in this position. On the other hand, an aggressive trader can work with this as well. They are able to spread it all out in order to get the most gains, even though it means there is a bigger loss potential if the stock does decline.

There are a few disadvantages that come with this strategy. As you can see with the examples we went through, the gains that you are able to earn are going to be limited. Sometimes, they may not be high enough to justify the risk of loss if your strategy doesn't work the way you want.

There can also be a significant amount of risk before you reach your expiry date, especially if the stock starts to slide. This could end with the trader having to pay a price that is too high or above the current price of the market for that stock. This risk is even higher if the difference that shows up between the short put and the long put strike prices are substantial.

As we talked about earlier, this kind of strategy is able to work out the best in any market that is trading sideways to marginally higher. This means that the range that works out best for this strategy is going to be limited compared to some of the other strategies. If the market surges, the trader will be better off buying a call or using a bull call spread. But if the market plunges, then this strategy will be really unprofitable.

The bull put spread is a suitable option strategy for helping you to earn a premium income or so you are able to purchase stocks effectively at prices that are below their market value. This strategy is going to have a limited amount of risk in the process and the potential gains can also be limited here, which is why there are some traders who choose not to work with this strategy at all.

CHAPTER 13:

∾

Strategy 6 – The Bear Put Spread

The final strategy we are going to look at here is the bear put spread, which is a good strategy to use when you think that the underlying asset is going to see a decline in its price. A bear put spread happens when the investor purchases some put options at a specific strike price, while also going through and selling the same number of puts with the same expiration date at a lower strike price. The highest amount that you are able to earn with this kind of strategy is the same as the difference that you see between the two strike prices. You will also need to minus the net cost of these options.

Let's take a look at an example of how this is going to work for you. Let's assume you see a stock that is trading at $30. An options trader is going to work with the bear put spread and can do this by purchasing one put option contract with a strike price at $35 for a cost of $475. They would then sell one of the put option contracts and have it listed with a strike price of $30 for $175 for all of the shares.

With this case, the investor ends up paying $300 for setting up the strategy. If you see that the underlying asset you chose closes below the $30 when the expiration happens, then the investor will get a profit that is equal to $200.

There are many different advantages that can happen when an investor chooses to work with the bear put spread. The main advantage is that the net risk of the trader is going to be reduced. Selling the put option with a strike price that is a bit lower is going to be important because it offsets some of the costs that you get for purchasing your put option that has the strike price that is higher.

This kind of strategy is going to carry a lot less risk compared to shorting the stock or the security, this is because the risk is limited to the net cost of your bear put spread. If you sell a stock short, there is theoretically an unlimited amount of risk if that stock does end up going higher.

If you are looking at that asset and you believe it is going to fall but the fall is done within a limited amount between when you purchase the asset and its expiration date, then the bear put spread is going to be the best play. But, if you think that the underlying asset is going to fall by a larger amount or it falls by a bigger amount than the trader set up, then you are going to lose the ability to claim any of the additional profit on this one. This is the trade-off you have to work with. You are able to reduce the amount of risk that you are dealing with, but your potential reward is going to be lower as well.

With the example that we were able to work with earlier, the profit from the bear put spread is going to max out if the underlying security ends up closing at the $30, which was the lower strike price you had purchased, at expiration. If it ends up closing below the $30, you will still earn the same amount of profit, no matter how much more it goes down by before that time.

However, if you notice that the price is going to close above the higher strike price, which we set at the $35 at that time, then there is going to be a loss on the move. This loss will end up being the entire amount that was spent to buy and get into that chosen spread.

Conclusion

Thanks for making it through to the end of *Options Trading Profit Playbook*. I hope it was informative and able to provide you with all of the tools you need to achieve your goals, whatever they may be.

The next step is to start putting some of the information we have discussed in this guidebook to good use. We have explored many of the different things you are able to do with this kind of trading, and some of the ways you can take advantage of any kind of market out there. There are a lot of neat things you can try out with options trading, but one of them is the fact that it can help you to earn a good profit, whether the market is doing well or going down.

This guidebook took some time to talk about the different aspects of options trading that you need to know. We explored what these types of contracts are all about and how you are able to make some good money on them. We talked about how you can benefit using these over investing in the regular stock market. We also took a bit of time to explore some of the terms and other information that you are going to need if you are interested in actually starting in this kind of market.

From there, we moved on to some of the things you need to know before doing your own trades, and a discussion on some actual trades that you may encounter along the way. At the end of this guidebook, we looked at some of the strategies you could consider working with if you were ready to get into an options contract and see just how much it can benefit you and all of the trading that you want to do.

There may be many different choices you can make out on the market when it comes to trading and seeing some great results with that. But options contracts and trading in options is one of the best to limit your risks and increase your profits. When you are ready to start working with options contracts and options trading, make sure you refer back to this guidebook to help you get started on the right path. This book comes complete with illustrations that explain the theories and strategies discussed with both options contracts and trading in options. This is to give you a better idea of how each one works and the benefits for each depending on the situation. It may be a bit daunting at first, but once you fully understand and you get to apply the concepts presented here, you will get to reap the benefits of trading.

Finally, if you found this book useful in any way, a review is always appreciated!